D1442587

189889

NORTH AMERICAN NATURAL RESOURCES

NATURAL GAS

North American Natural Resources

Coal

Copper

Freshwater Resources

Gold and Silver

Iron

Marine Resources

Natural Gas

Oil

Renewable Energy

Salt

Timber and Forest Products

Uranium

NATURAL GAS

Steve Parker

MASON CREST

Mason Crest
450 Parkway Drive, Suite D
Broomall, PA 19008
www.masoncrest.com

MTM Publishing, Inc.
435 West 23rd Street, #8C
New York, NY 10011
www.mtmpublishing.com

President: Valerie Tomaselli
Vice President, Book Development: Hilary Poole
Designer: Annemarie Redmond
Illustrator: Richard Garratt
Copyeditor: Peter Jaskowiak
Editorial Assistant: Andrea St. Aubin

Series ISBN: 978-1-4222-3378-8
ISBN: 978-1-4222-3385-6
Ebook ISBN: 978-1-4222-8559-6

Library of Congress Cataloging-in-Publication Data
Parker, Steve, 1952-
  Natural gas / by Steve Parker.
      pages cm. — (North American natural resources)
  Includes bibliographical references and index.
  ISBN 978-1-4222-3385-6 (hardback) — ISBN 978-1-4222-3378-8 (series) — ISBN
978-1-4222-8559-6 (ebook)
 1. Natural gas—Juvenile literature. 2. Gas as fuel—Juvenile literature. 3. Hydraulic fracturing—
Juvenile literature. 4. Natural gas—Environmental aspects—Juvenile literature. I. Title.
 TP350.P325 2015
 553.2'85—dc23
                                        2015005847

Printed and bound in the United States of America.

First printing
9 8 7 6 5 4 3 2 1

TABLE OF CONTENTS

Key Icons to Look for:

 Words to Understand: These words with their easy-to-understand definitions will increase the reader's understanding of the text, while building vocabulary skills.

 Sidebars: This boxed material within the main text allows readers to build knowledge, gain insights, explore possibilities, and broaden their perspectives by weaving together additional information to provide realistic and holistic perspectives.

 Research Projects: Readers are pointed toward areas of further inquiry connected to each chapter. Suggestions are provided for projects that encourage deeper research and analysis.

 Text-Dependent Questions: These questions send the reader back to the text for more careful attention to the evidence presented there.

 Series Glossary of Key Terms: This back-of-the-book glossary contains terminology used throughout the series. Words found here increase the reader's ability to read and comprehend higher-level books and articles in this field.

Note to Educator: As publishers, we feel it's our role to give young adults the tools they need to thrive in a global society. To encourage a more worldly perspective, this book contains both imperial and metric measurements as well as references to a wider global context. We hope to expose the readers to the most common conversions they will come across outside of North America.

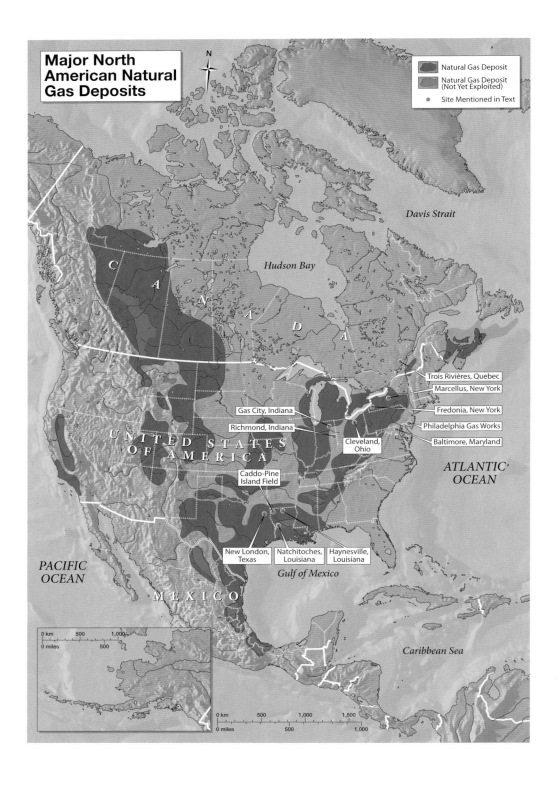

Major North
American Natural
Gas Deposits

Natural Gas Deposit
Natural Gas Deposit
(Not Yet Exploited)
● Site Mentioned in Text

N

Davis Strait

C A N A D A

Hudson Bay

Trois Rivières, Quebec
Marcellus, New York
Gas City, Indiana
Fredonia, New York
Richmond, Indiana
Philadelphia Gas Works
Cleveland, Ohio
Baltimore, Maryland

U N I T E D S T A T E S
O F A M E R I C A

ATLANTIC OCEAN

Caddo-Pine Island Field

PACIFIC OCEAN

New London, Texas
Natchitoches, Louisiana
Haynesville, Louisiana

Gulf of Mexico

M E X I C O

Caribbean Sea

0 km   500   1,000
0 miles   500

0 km   500   1,000   1,500
0 miles   500   1,000

INTRODUCTION

Gas is many things. This word can mean gasoline for auto engines. It can also refer to any substance that is neither solid nor liquid, but in a gaseous state—like gases in the air around us. Gas can also be a gaseous fuel that is burned for many purposes—to generate electricity, cook, heat homes and buildings, make light in gas lamps, and power vehicles, to name a few.

This book uses the last meaning of the word gas. More precisely, it is about *natural gas*. The important and valuable resource of natural gas

A fracking rig in a Colorado field. (Lonnyinco/Dreamstime)

is a mix of gaseous substances found naturally deep in the ground. The North American continent has huge amounts, or reserves, of natural gas. The United States ranks 5th in the list of nations with most natural gas reserves, and Canada is also in the top 20.

Natural gas, petroleum oil (usually just called oil), and coal make up the "Big Three" fossil fuels. They were formed from the preserved remains, or fossils, of living things that thrived and died millions of years ago. The processes that made natural gas are similar to those that formed petroleum oil, and these two resources are often found together. Their drilling, extraction, transport, and processing (or refining) also have many similarities. So the natural gas and petroleum oil industries are closely linked, and many big companies deal in both.

Natural gas burns in a "cleaner" way—that is, with less pollution—than coal or oil fuels such as gasoline, diesel, and kerosene. In addition, its world stores, or reserves, are expected to last more than 250 years, which is longer than coal or petroleum oil. About one-quarter of North America's energy needs are filled by natural gas and its products, and more than 19/20ths of this is produced on the North American continent itself. So the natural gas business in North America is less at risk from problems with world energy supplies, which can be affected by many events, such as wars or terrorist attacks.

Even though natural gas has some advantages over other fossil fuels, it still contributes greatly to climate change. Drilling, extraction, transport, and storage cause various forms of pollution and bring safety hazards like fires and explosions. Fracking, a process of extracting oil or gas from rock formations deep in the ground, has many of its own concerns. Also, gas is not renewable. It is a precious resource, and its use is growing, but it is probably not a long-term solution to future energy needs.

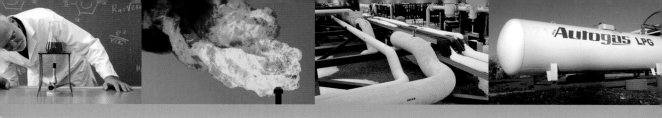

Chapter One

HOW NATURAL GAS FORMED

atural gas started life millions of years ago, as microscopic life forms known as plankton, floating in large bodies of water such as seas, oceans, and great lakes. Some of these life forms were phytoplankton (plant plankton). Just like other plants, the phytoplankton captured the Sun's light energy to grow through the process called photosynthesis. These phytoplankton were consumed by zooplankton (animal plankton), which took in the Sun's energy for their own use. Some of the larger zooplankton ate up the smaller ones, transferring the sun's energy again, and so on.

Words to Understand

hydrocarbon: a substance containing only the pure chemical substances, or elements, carbon and hydrogen.

kerogens: a variety of substances formed when once-living things decayed and broke down, on the way to becoming natural gas or oil.

methanogenic: able to make the gas methane.

porous: allowing a liquid to seep or soak through small holes and channels, like a sponge.

shales: rocks with very small particles or grains, usually of clay minerals.

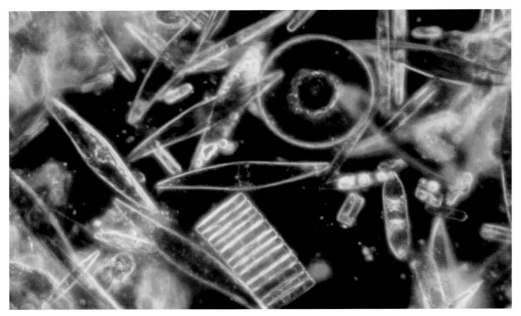

Phytoplankton viewed through a microscope. These are called diatoms; they are the most common type of phytoplankton.

Usually, when living things die, they are scavenged and rot away, and the minerals and other substances from their bodies are recycled naturally into new life. At certain times in the distant past, however, in warm shallow waters with plenty of nutrients and minerals, decay and recycling did not happen fast enough. As a result, dead remains began to accumulate on the bottoms of seas and lakes. As they piled up, low-oxygen conditions meant that certain kinds of microbes, called **methanogenic** bacteria, could thrive. They managed to rot and break down some of the remains of living things, producing methane gas in the process.

The lower layers of rotting remains were gradually squeezed harder and harder by the weight of more layers above; this pressure raised their temperature, too. As the layers gradually turned into rock, what was left of the plankton broke down even further, being essentially "slow cooked" by a process called catagenesis. They formed substances called **kerogens**, which have a slimy or waxy nature. Kerogens are made of the two chemical substances (elements) hydrogen (H) and carbon (C). So they are known as **hydrocarbons**.

Breakdown into Natural Gas

What happened to the kerogens depended on depth of burial, which determined the pressure and temperature. From about 120 up to 300°F (50–150°C), they became petroleum oil. This temperature range is known as the *oil window*, with most oil formation at 140–250°F (60–120°C). Being buried even deeper meant the kerogens got hotter still. From 212 to 390°F (100–200°C), equivalent to being about 4 miles (6.4 kilometers) deep, the kerogen breakdown yielded natural gas. In North America, about one-quarter of natural gas reserves are known as *associated gas*, meaning the gas occurs together with petroleum oil. The other three-quarters are nonassociated, existing mainly without oil.

Natural gas, like petroleum oil, varies in its contents. Usually, it is mainly methane, ranging from 75 to 98 percent, but more generally it is 90–95 percent methane. Most of the rest is the gases ethane, typically at levels of 2.5–3 percent; propane, at 0.2 percent; and butane, at less than 0.1 percent. The amount of carbon dioxide varies greatly but is usually less than 1 percent. There are also small quantities of nitrogen (1–5 percent), as well as hydrogen sulfide, oxygen, hydrogen, and water vapor.

The Passing of Time

The processes that made natural gas and petroleum oil took millions of years and happened only in certain places. Burial to greater depths caused more natural gas

Types of Natural Gas

- "Dry" natural gas is nearly all methane, whether natural from the ground or having been purified.
- "Wet" natural gas is less pure, with the other gases like ethane, propane, and butane mixed in, as natural gas liquids, or NGLs.
- "Sour" natural gas contains significant amounts of hydrogen sulfide, which can eat away or corrode equipment and produce polluting sulfur-containing gases when it is burned.
- "Sweet" natural gas has very little hydrogen sulfide.

to form, compared to petroleum oil. Then, over millions more years, great earth movements, drifting continents, erosion, mountain building, and similar actions altered the overlying rocks. This is why natural gas and petroleum oil are found at varying depths today. Because they formed from the preserved or fossilized remains of living things, they are known as fossil fuels. Other terms include hydrocarbon fuels and organic fuels, since they were made naturally or organically.

Where natural gas and petroleum oil would collect depended on the nature of the rocks. These needed to be **porous**, with tiny channels and holes. The natural gas and oil could ooze through, like water soaking through a sponge. Being light in weight, or low density, natural gas and oil tended to flow or migrate upward through porous rock, usually until they reached a rock layer that was nonporous or solid. Here they stayed, trapped under this layer.

A cross-section view of shale.

These valuable areas of natural gas and petroleum oil are known as gas fields and oil fields. They do not exist as large "bubbles" of gas or "lakes" of oil, with rocks around. They are held in the cavities or pores in the rock, just as a sponge holds water. Porous rocks where this happens include sandstones and types of limestone with relatively big particles, called coarse-grained sandstones. **Shales** also contain enormous amounts of gas and oil. Shales have smaller or finer grains, so they hold their contents more tightly, which is why high-pressure cracking or fracking is needed to extract the natural gas and oil.

Where and When Natural Gas Formed

For millions of years, large areas of North America were covered by seas and oceans. Here the conditions were suitable for natural gas and petroleum oil formation. The main regions for natural gas were the Canadian Arctic Islands; the Northern Frontier of northwestern Alaska and the adjacent Northwest Territories; eastern Canada's Atlantic states; the Rockies

North American Gas Fields

The vast Marcellus Shale gas fields cover an area of more than 100,000 square miles (260,000 square kilometers) in Pennsylvania and West Virginia, and into bordering Ohio, New York, Maryland, and Virginia. It probably contains more than 100 trillion cubic feet (2.8 trillion cubic meters) of natural gas in its shale rocks (some estimates go much higher). Almost as much is in the Haynesville Shale gas fields, with an area of about 10,000 square miles (26,000 square kilometers) in southwestern Arkansas, northeastern Texas, and northwestern Louisiana.

Natural gas drilling operation in Haynesville, Louisiana.

in British Columbia and Alberta south and east to Utah and Colorado; the US heartland around Kansas, Oklahoma, and Texas; the eastern Midwest from the Great Lakes south to Tennessee; and the Gulf Coast and northern Gulf of Mexico.

Natural gas and petroleum oil formation have been going on for more than 1,000 million years. Much of the natural gas used today is from 400 to 250 million years ago, and from 180 to 15 million years ago. For example, the huge Marcellus Shale natural gas reserves date back to 390–380 million years ago.

Exposed shale outside Marcellus, New York.

Methane in Space

Methane is a common gas on some planets and moons in deep space. It was once believed that outer space was the only place to find methane hydrates, because it is cold enough there for water to freeze into ice, gathering up methane from the atmosphere. But the 1960s, scientists looking for natural gas fields found methane hydrates under the frozen land of Siberia, and in the 1980s, they found them under the deep mud and ooze of Earth's ocean floor.

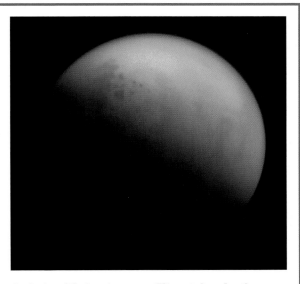

A photo of Saturn's moon, Titan, taken by the Cassini spacecraft. The darker areas are hydrocarbon lakes, made of ethane and methane.

Methane Hydrates

The main natural gas, methane, is also found in a very different form as methane hydrates (methane clathrates). These are, in effect, methane mixed with water in the form of crystals; they are also known as methane ice, fire ice, or solid natural gas. Methane hydrates are found in huge amounts in the seabed, and also under the always-frozen ground called permafrost, in the far north of the world.

Methane hydrates were made as methane from far below, formed as described above, oozed up to the surface. Here it met extremely cold water at immensely high pressure. The two mixed to form ice-like crystals full of methane. If these are warmed up, or if the pressure is reduced, the methane comes out as a gas. One cubic foot (20 liters) of the crystals can yield 150 cubic feet (4,250 liters) of gaseous methane.

The amounts of methane hydrates are staggering. Worldwide, they could contain more energy than the world's natural gas, oil, and coal added together. Several nations, including the United States and Canada, are testing whether methane hydrates could become a useable fuel in the future, as explained on later pages.

TEXT-DEPENDENT QUESTIONS

1. What are the main gaseous substances in natural gas?
2. At what kinds of temperatures did natural gas form?
3. Which types of rocks are best at holding natural gas?

RESEARCH PROJECTS

1. Look up some information on phytoplankton and zooplankton, and also the names of different kinds. Try researching diatoms and dinoflagellates.
2. Find out more about methane hydrates. Do they form at particular places in the ocean floor, such as around the edges of the shallow areas called continental shelves?

Chapter Two

EXTRACTION

Natural gas and petroleum oil companies spend millions of dollars to find and extract Earth's natural resources. Often, they work in the world's harshest environments, such as the frozen far north, scorching barren deserts, windswept rocky uplands, and the stormy open ocean. Vital to the quest are experts known as geologists. They study the Earth, what it is made of, soil and rocks, and how these form and wear away. There are also surveyors, who measure and record the shape of the land with its hills, valleys, mountains, canyons, plains, rivers, and lakes. Together, these and other experts search for signs that an area might have valuable resources beneath the surface.

Words to Understand

hydraulics: the science and engineering of fluids and their properties, such as how they flow under pressure.

refine: separating gas and oil into their separate pure substances or ingredients.

remote sensing: detecting and gathering information from a distance, such as when satellites in space measure air and ground temperature below.

seismology: the study of waves, as vibrations or "shaking," that pass through Earth's rocks, soils, and other structures.

The Search for Natural Gas

Many methods are used when searching, or prospecting, for natural gas and oil. Sources of information include photographs taken by satellites in space and aerial surveys by aircraft. Gaining information like this from a distance is known as **remote sensing**. The searchers may also drive or walk around an area to get detailed measurements and samples of soil and rocks. They look for certain types

An aerial GIS map of part of Texas. GIS stands for geographic information systems.

and ages of rocks that could signal natural gas or oil below. Rocks are dated by the fossils they contain. They are identified by their mineral makeup, physical features such as grain size, and chemical reactions with acids and other substances.

Many other features and measurements are explored. Earth's natural downward pull of gravity varies slightly, since natural gas and oil are lighter or less dense that solid rock, reducing the force of gravity by a tiny amount. Instruments known as gravimeters detect

> ## Boring Facts
>
> The deepest boreholes go down to depths of more than 40,000 feet (12,200 meters)—that's over 7 miles (11 kilometers). Since the hole may go at an angle or bend, it's actual length is even greater. At sea the boreholes can go down more than 30,000 feet (9 kilometers) below sea level.

these changes. Similarly, the force of Earth's natural magnetic field varies, and this variation is measured by magnetometers. Also, the way that rocks carry electricity can give valuable clues. This is determined by a process known as electromagnetic surveying. Another method is to use sensitive "sniffer" machines that can detect the faintest traces of natural gas or oil vapors coming up into the air.

When exploring the shallow seabed, divers may go down to take samples and make measurements. Or, especially in deep water, underwater vehicles called submersibles can carry out these tasks.

A very important technique is **seismology**, which examines the way vibrations or shock waves pass through rocks and other substances. This is most dramatic during earth tremors and earthquakes. Exploring for natural resources involves making "microquakes" using small controlled explosions or heavy weights bashed onto the ground by "thumpers." The presence of natural gas and oil alters the way the seismic waves travel, and these alterations can be picked up at various distances by seismometers.

Together, all these techniques allow geologists, geophysicists, surveyors, and others to make three-dimensional maps of the ground and rocks below, showing suspected deposits of natural gas and oil. For example, natural gas often occurs in certain kinds of shale rock formations known as "plays." If the signs look good, the decision is made to drill exploratory boreholes.

The semi-submersible rig, *Deepsea Delta*, drilling for gas and oil in the North Sea.

Drilling for Natural Gas

Boreholes cannot be drilled anywhere. Permission is needed from landowners or other authorities, whether on land (onshore) or at sea (offshore). If a search hits big reserves of natural gas or oil, these could be worth billions, or even trillions, of dollars. There must be legal contracts showing who is involved and how the profits should be shared.

The company doing the exploring organizes the drilling rigs with all their accompanying equipment, such as generators, fuel, accommodation for the workers, food and facilities, transport trucks, supply ships, aircraft, and helicopters. Simply setting up a drilling camp costs massive amounts of money, especially if the site is in a remote, hard-to-reach area, like rugged hills, thick jungle, or the open ocean.

Drilling is a tough process centered on a very hard-working piece of machinery, the drill bit. The drill bit rotates so that its teeth grind away and eat into even the hardest rock. Hammer bits also use a banging or pounding action to smash up the rock. The drill bit is made of the toughest materials, such as tungsten carbide or a coating of tiny diamonds. It is on the end of a tube or pipe that is gripped around its ridged or flattened portion, the kelly, and turned around by a turntable or rotary platform. The pipe hangs inside a tall tower, the derrick.

As the drill bit spins, it drills or bores a hole down into the ground. As it goes deeper, it is hoisted up inside the derrick, another length of pipe is screwed on the upper end, and the new extended pipe is lowered to drill further down. This happens again and again, with the lengthening line of screwed-together pipes forming the drill string that spins the drill bit at its lower end.

Valuable Mud

If the drill bit simply scraped at the solid rock by itself, it would soon get too hot, worn, and clogged with ground-off bits of rock, called cuttings. So a special fluid called "mud"—mostly water with various chemicals added—is pumped at high pressure down inside the drill string. This squirts out through holes in the drill bit and then flows back up between the drill string and the side of the borehole. The continually flowing mud cools the drill bit, lubricates it to reduce friction and wear, and also carries away the cuttings. At the surface, the mud is cleaned to use again, and the cuttings are analyzed to check the rock the drill bit has reached.

The depth of a natural gas borehole ranges from less than 1,000 feet (300 meters) to more than 30,000 feet (6 miles, or 9 kilometers) under the land, and more than 10,000 feet (2 miles or 3 kilometers) beneath the seabed.

A natural gas well in the Lost Hills Oil Field, San Joaquin Valley, California.

Hitting the Target

Natural gas or oil may be under such enormous pressure that they suddenly burst up the borehole and blast out at the surface. This is called a blowout. To prevent such an occurrence, a blowout preventer has various valves and seals to control the pressure. The next task is completion—or getting the borehole ready for steady production. This involves removing the drill string, installing production casing, cementing around it, and then "perfing"—making small holes or perforations with a device called a perforation gun. The natural gas is usually under high pressure in the rocks, so it flows all the way up to the surface.

Where the borehole meets the surface, called the wellhead, more equipment is installed. A set of branching pipes, tubes, valves, and dials—called a "Christmas tree"—is used to monitor and control the flow. The natural gas is led away along pipes to a local storage area for the next stage.

Horizontal Drilling and Fracking

Two recent technologies have greatly increased natural gas and oil extraction. One is horizontal or directional drilling—being able to steer the drill bit so the borehole follows a curved path. The first part of the borehole is drilled straight as usual. When it reaches a depth called the kick-off point, the regular drill string is removed and replaced with a new set-up that can tilt the drill bit. The borehole bends or curves around from vertical to horizontal, so that it travels within the layer of rocks

This 3D model shows how horizontal fracturing forces the release of natural gas trapped deep underground.

Pipelines

The TransCanada Pipeline was completed in 1958. It takes natural gas from Alberta to Quebec, a distance of just over 2,000 miles (3,200 kilometers). The Rockies Express Pipeline or REX, almost 1,700 miles (2,700 kilometers) long, runs from the Rocky Mountains in Colorado to eastern Ohio. It was finished in 2009. The Transcontinental Pipeline between the Texan Gulf Coast and New York is almost as long.

containing natural gas or oil. Several holes can fan out into the rock layer from one drilling site at the surface, reaching far more of the resource than drilling straight down.

Another recent technology is called **hydraulic** fracturing, or *fracking*. This process is used for natural gas or oil that is held firmly within very fine-grained rocks, especially shales. A fluid mixture of water, small particles such as sand or man-made ceramics, and chemicals is forced down at incredibly high pressure. It pushes its way into the rock, creating cracks or fractures. A typical well needs more than 1 million gallons (3.78 million liters) of water for the fracking fluid, equivalent to more than 200 big tanker trucks full of water. The high-pressure fracking takes several days, and then the pressure is reduced so the natural gas or oil can flow up to the surface. Fracking extracts natural gas or oil from rocks that previously would not release them, and from wells had "run dry" using older methods.

The United States has more than 30,000 natural gas wells, and that number is rising fast. Around the world, up to 20,000 new gas wells are drilled each year, mostly for fracking.

Transporting Natural Gas

After extraction, natural gas may be **refined** on site, at the wellheads, or later at another site, as explained in the next chapter. Natural gas is transported in two main ways: as a gas or as a liquid.

Large, long-distance pipelines are known as transmission pipelines. At their ends are smaller distribution pipelines that carry the natural gas to power generators, factories, and homes. The United States has more than 200 main natural gas pipeline networks with over 320,000 miles (515,000 kilometers) of transmission pipes in the lower 48 states, plus another 50,000-plus miles (8,000 kilometers) in Canada and up to Alaska. The vast, branching system of distribution pipelines totals more than 2 million miles (over 3 million kilometers).

Main transmission pipelines are usually made of steel and range from about 20 to 42 inches (50 to 107 centimeters) in diameter. As they snake across the scenery, the natural gas is pushed through them by a network of some 1,500 compressor or pumping stations. The natural gas is at pressures of 1,000 pounds per square inch (70 kilograms per square centimeter) or more—30 to 40 times more than air in a regular automobile tire.

Natural gas pipelines.

The second main way of transporting natural gas is to cool it so it changes from a gas into a liquid, called liquefied natural gas (LNG). This happens at around −260°F (−160°C), when the methane shrinks in volume 600 times, making it much smaller and easier to put into containers. First, the natural gas is cleaned of problem substances such as dust, water, and acids. Then it is cooled in stages using industrial versions of domestic refrigerators, until it becomes a liquid. It must be kept this cold during its transport, so it is put in special trucks, railroad wagons, barges, or big ships known as LNG carriers. These specialized ocean-going vessels have several huge ball-shaped tanks or flasks. The LNG is pumped in after the tanks are first cooled and made safe to prevent any explosions or fires.

Gas on the High Seas

The first liquefied natural gas (LNG) carrier took its cargo from the Gulf of Mexico to Britain in 1959. With the growth of natural gas use around the world, there are now more than 400 LNG carriers, and more are being built. The biggest can hold 10 million cubic feet (285,000 cubic meters) of LNG, weighing over 110,000 tons (100,000 metric tons).

A US Coast Guard boat beside the massive LNG tanker *Berge Boston*, in 2006.

TEXT-DEPENDENT QUESTIONS

1. What are some of the devices and measurements used to find natural gas fields?
2. What are the functions of drilling "mud"?
3. How cold is natural gas when it turns into liquid, and why is this done?

RESEARCH PROJECTS

1. Find out about the designs and materials of drill bits, and research terms such as *fixed cutter* and *roller cone*. Have designs changed much over the years?
2. How is liquefied natural gas kept so cold on its long ocean voyages in LNG carrier ships?

Chapter Three

USES

Words to Understand

by-product: a substance or material that is not the main desired product of a process, but happens to be made along the way.

catalyst: a substance that speeds up a chemical change or reaction that would otherwise happen slowly, if at all.

renewable: a substance that can be made, or a process used, again and again.

synthesis: making or producing something by adding substances together.

By far, the greatest use of natural gas is for heating. Natural gas warms buildings, provides hot water, and cooks food. It is also used in firing kilns for ceramics, in plastics and chemicals production, in steel mills, and of course, for electricity generation.

When burned as an energy resource, natural gas provides some 27 percent of the total energy used in North America. Petroleum oil is the source of the most energy, supplying around 35 percent (especially for transport), while coal comes in at 19 percent. Renewables such as hydropower (from hydroelectric dams), solar, wind, and biogas supply about 10 percent, and nuclear power supplies 8 percent. In the next 20–30 years, natural gas and **renewables** should rise to supply about half of all North American energy.

A natural gas-fired power plant.

About one-third of the energy from natural gas is used for electricity production—which itself consumes two-fifths of all energy used in North America. Another one-third goes to factories and industries. The final one-third is burned by residential properties such as houses and apartments, and by commercial set-ups like offices, restaurants and stores. Less than 1 percent is burned for transportation in vehicles fuelled by natural gas.

Ingredients in Natural Gas

Like petroleum oil, natural gas is refined into its various parts or ingredients. The main ingredient is methane. Other gaseous ingredients are propane, butane, and similar substances, which also usually become fuels. Further ingredients that come

Propane is a by-product of natural gas that is often used for cooking.

straight from the well may include water vapor, nitrogen, helium, carbon dioxide, and hydrogen sulfide. Hydrogen sulfide causes an eating away, or corrosion, of gas equipment, and water vapor brings with it the problem of methane hydrates, as described in chapter five.

According to the amounts of these ingredients, there may be enough of them to sell to their own chemical industries. But some natural gas processing plants are in such remote places that transporting these **by-products** for further use costs more than they are worth. Like flare gas, also described later, this represents a great waste of natural resources.

Processing Natural Gas

Refining or processing natural gas is based on changing temperature and pressure as the gas travels through a maze of pipes, chambers, tanks, tubes, valves, towers, boilers, condensers and distillers. Each of the substances in natural gas has its own boiling point, at which turns from liquid into gas (this is the same temperature as its condensing point, at which it changes from gas to liquid). Methane, for example, boils at −257.8°F (−164°C), while propane does so at −44°F (−42°C), and butane at 30 to 34°F (−1 to 1°C). But these temperatures change, going down with reduced pressure and up with increased pressure. So, by arranging a series of containers or towers with different temperatures and pressures, the various ingredients, or fractions, of natural gas boil off or condense out at different points. Here they can be collected in pure form. This general process of boiling and then condensing, which is also done for petroleum oil, is called fractional distillation.

Also used in processing are materials called membranes, as well as substances known as **catalysts**. Membranes are sheets of tailor-made materials with holes and channels of a precise size. These may work as "molecular sieves," allowing some molecules to pass through and holding back others. Catalysts speed up (or slow down) a chemical change or reaction, without themselves being altered at the end. They can be added to membranes, coated onto grids, or mixed in as powder or gas.

In pure form, the methane, propane, butane, and similar parts of natural gases are odorless. Before they reach consumers, tiny amounts of substances called odorants are added that have strong, distinctive scents. These chemicals include various mercaptans or thiols (with a garlic-like odor) and hydrogen sulfide ("rotten eggs"). The odorants enables people to smell a gas leak and act quickly.

Liquefied Gas Products

Natural gas pipelines deliver a fuel that is almost all methane. The burnable gases such as propane and butane—which are also obtained from refining oil—are separated to become liquefied petroleum gas (LPG). In this form, they take up far less space: propane, for example, "shrinks" 250 times when compressed from gaseous to liquid form. LPG is put in tanker trucks, and into metal bottles and cylinders, for a multitude of uses, such as heating and cooking. It also goes by a multitude of names, such as bottled gas, barbecue gas, and camping gas.

A growing use for LPG is autogas—usually a propane-butane mix. It is a relatively clean-burning fuel, producing less pollution than gasoline or diesel. Also, compared to those fuels, autogas produces about one-sixth less carbon dioxide.

Sulfur from Natural Gas

Hydrogen sulfide from natural gas can be converted by the Claus process into the pure substance or element sulfur. The hydrogen sulfide is heated to more than 1,500°F (820°C), and it is then treated with catalysts. From natural gas, petroleum oil, and coal, the Claus process yields 90 million tons (over 80 million metric tons) of sulfur each year—and sulfur is one of the most widely used substances in the chemical industry.

Autogas

The use of autogas fuel is rising in some regions, from Italy, Poland, and Turkey to South Korea and Australia. In particular, it is favored for use in city vehicle fleets, such as taxicabs and delivery trucks, which can refuel at their own purpose-built "gas" stations. In the United States, some cities are increasingly using natural gas as fuel for public buses.

Natural gas-powered transportation at the Grand Canyon Visitor Center.

Plastics and GTL

Ethane, another gas found in some natural gas, goes a different route. Along with the ethane produced when refining petroleum oil, its main use is to make ethene or ethylene, which is turned into polyethylene (or polythene)—the world's most common plastic. It is used to wrap up all kinds of products, from foods to automobile parts, and to make plastic bags, refuse sacks, plastic bottles, and construction materials. Ethane is also used by the chemical industry to make products such as acetic acid, more commonly known as vinegar.

Natural gas can also be converted to oil-like liquids and fuels, using gas-to-liquid (GTL) technology. Like natural gas processing, these methods employ heat and cold, pressure, and catalysts. The Fischer-Tropsch process begins with methane and ends

Polyethylene has a huge variety of uses, including packaging and bottles.

with the gases carbon dioxide, carbon monoxide, and hydrogen, plus water. The carbon dioxide, monoxide, and hydrogen go to form syngas (**synthesis** gas), which can then be made into synthetic natural gas (SNG). *Syngas* can also be converted into liquid fuels like methanol. In yet another possible route, methanol and syngas are used to produce gasoline. All of these conversions show how complicated and interlinked the natural gas and petroleum oil industries have become.

Supply and Demand

Natural gas takes up vast volumes when stored, but it requires lots of energy to cool or compress into a liquid, and both methods present safety risks. It is stored in various ways, such as injecting it back into old wells or depleted gas reservoirs, or storing it in caverns once occupied by salt deep underground.

Balancing production with demand is a giant juggling act. Since so much natural gas goes to electricity generators, gas production must look ahead to ramp up production for times when electricity is in high demand, such as cold winters, when it is used for electrical heating, or hot spells, when it is used for air conditioning.

When the need for electricity rises rapidly, generators of the gas turbine type, fuelled by natural gas, can be "switched on" much faster than those powered by coal, oil, or nuclear fuel. These fast-response generators are called peaking power plants, or "peaker plants." They kick in when electricity demand is high (at a peak), sometimes even for just a few hours, then ramp down again until the next time they are needed. Peaker plants add their electricity to the regular amounts produced by the big, continuously running power plants.

Other products from natural gas are hydrogen; substances used in aerosol sprays, refrigerators, and freezers; and ammonia and similar nitrogen-rich chemicals for fertilizers. The petrochemical industry is so huge and interwoven that natural gas substances can also be converted into products usually associated with petroleum oil—not only gasoline and plastics, as mentioned above, but also paints, pharmaceuticals, synthetic textiles, and dozens of others.

Natural gas storage tanks in Nanaimo, British Columbia.

TEXT-DEPENDENT QUESTIONS

1. What is the main gas in natural gas, and what is its chief use?
2. What are some of the physical and chemical processes used in processing natural gas?
3. What are GTL and SNG, and how are they linked?

RESEARCH PROJECTS

1. Gather information on how sulfur-containing substances damage all kinds of equipment and cause pollution, and how this is prevented.
2. Find out more about autogas. Where is it most popular, and what are its advantages and drawbacks compared to gasoline and diesel fuels?

Chapter Four

THE NATURAL GAS INDUSTRY

In 1816, Baltimore, Maryland, became the first North American city to used piped gas for street lamps. This followed the fashion in Europe for gas street lighting, but as in Europe, the fuel was coal or town gas, made from coal. Its use spread rapidly and soon many towns built their own gas lamp networks.

Words to Understand

alloy: a combination or mixture of a metal with another substance, which may be a metal or non-metal, for example, the metal iron and the non-metal carbon make the alloy steel.

combustion: burning by combining with oxygen.

flare: a flame that burns fast and brightly.

municipal: to do with a town or district.

recession: in business and industry, a lessening of trade and work and profits.

In 1821, in Fredonia, New York, a local gunsmith named William Hart combined natural gas seeps and coal gas lighting. He dug a well at a nearby bubbling gas seep, and the natural gas was sent via a pipeline of hollow logs to light an inn on the Buffalo-Cleveland stagecoach route. This was one of the first commercial uses of natural gas in North America. More natural gas wells were then drilled, Fredonia became famous, and the natural gas fashion spread.

In 1836, Philadelphia established a natural gas distribution system, the Philadelphia Gas Works, that lit 46 lamps along the city's main street. The system came under **municipal** ownership in 1841 and still supplies gas today. Meanwhile, back in Fredonia, in 1858, local business people set up the first natural gas company in the United States, which also supplied clean water to the town—the Fredonia Gas Light and Water Works Company.

Light and Heat

A few years earlier, in 1854, a gadget had been invented that would radically change gas use. In Heidelberg University, in Germany, coal gas lighting was in common use for lighting, as it was in many other places. The gas burned with a gentle yellow flame as it came out of an opening, mixing with the air around it to get the oxygen needed for **combustion**. The chemist Robert Bunsen, however, wanted a hotter flame that was more suited to heating chemicals in his laboratory. His idea was to mix the gas with air beforehand, so there that more oxygen would be available at the actual burning, making the flame much hotter.

The result was the Bunsen burner now familiar in so many laboratories and science classrooms around the world. The invention was a key factor in using gas for heat. The invention soon led to similar, bigger burner designs for heating systems, ovens, boilers, furnaces, and kilns.

A Pioneer Energy Company

In 1857 the Fredonia Gas Works and Water Company stated its aim: "By boring down to slate rock and sinking to sufficient depth to penetrate the manufactories of nature; thus to collect from her laboratories the natural gas and purify it; to furnish the citizens with good, cheap light."

Bunsen burners are common sights in any chemistry class.

In 1882, Thomas Edison's company opened the first central electricity generating plant at Pearl Street Station in New York City. The power supplied 80 customers and 400 electric lights along the block. This method of lighting spelled the beginning of the end for gas lamps in many towns and cities.

Gas Boom and Bust

During the early years of drilling for petroleum oil, the natural gas that came with it was usually regarded as a nuisance. It was therefore simply let go—vented into the air or burned as a **flare**. One of the earliest pipelines to carry natural gas for use elsewhere was built in 1853 in Canada. Made of cast iron, it took the gas about 15 miles (24 kilometers) to Trois Rivières, Quebec.

Natural gas being flared (or burned) off at the Orvis State Well in North Dakota.

In the United States, in 1876, drillers discovered what would become the Trenton natural gas field in eastern Indiana, bordering Ohio. After a slow start, industries realized that there was so much natural gas that it was far from a nuisance. By the mid-1880s, factories and facilities were moving in to use the natural gas as heating fuel to produce iron, steel, and other metals, as well as glass, rubber, and other major products. Indiana's tradition of heavy industry grew as a result. In 1891, one of the first long-distance natural gas pipelines took gas from central Indiana some 120 miles (195 kilometers) to Chicago. In 1892, the town of Harrisburg, near the center of one of the rich sources, even changed its name to Gas City. Spare natural gas was burned constantly in great displays known as flambeaux.

> ## The Largest US Natural Gas Producers
>
> Many big energy companies produce both petroleum oil and natural gas. This ranking of US-based companies is for worldwide natural gas production.
>
> 1. Exxon Mobil
> 2. Chevron
> 3. ConocoPhillips
> 4. Devon Energy
> 5. XTO Energy
> 6. Chesapeake Energy
> 7. Anadarko Petroleum
> 8. EOG Resources
> 9. Williams Companies
> 10. Marathon Oil

But the Indiana gas boom did not last. More than two-thirds of the gas was wasted and burned in flambeaux. By the early 1900s, the state's heavy industries had to either look for another fuel or move to another state. Most chose to stay and convert to coal. This pattern of boom and bust was repeated in other regions across Ohio, Pennsylvania, and New York, and south to West Virginia.

Pipelines and Networks

In 1901, the famous oil "gusher" at Spindletop, East Texas, began the great Texas oil boom and the rapid growth of the petroleum industry. Natural gas fields were also located in the area, but constructing long-distance, high-pressure natural gas pipelines was difficult. The Caddo-Pine Island Field of oil and natural gas was discovered in northwestern Louisiana in 1905, and the next year a natural gas pipeline was built to

Spindletop oil wells in Port Arthur, Texas, photographed around 1901.

Shreveport, about 25 miles (40 kilometers) away. Still, much natural gas was "flared" at the well site.

Canada continued to construct several natural gas pipelines. These included Canadian Western Natural Gas's 1912 line from Bow Island to Calgary, Alberta, a distance of some 170 miles (275 kilometers). In 1923, Northwestern Utilities Limited finished a 77-mile (124-kilometer) natural gas pipeline from Viking to Edmonton, Alberta. But, in general, the limited engineering and technology of the time prevented large-scale pipeline networks.

During and soon after World War II, there were advances in making various kinds of metals and **alloys**, in welding metals together, and in methods of rolling long lengths of pipe. These made high-pressure pipelines less costly and safer to build and operate. Long-distance gas pipelines soon began to wind their way across North America—a trend that continued into the 1950s and 1960s. These pipelines made more natural gas more available in more places. In homes it was used for cooking, heating, and hot water. In industry, it was the new fuel for processing plants, chemical works, furnaces and boilers, and electricity generation.

With the advances of horizontal drilling and fracking, the natural gas industry is currently going through another major boom. Estimates predict that shale natural gas will increase from around two-fifths of natural gas production in the United States, to almost three-fifths by the year 2040. At that time the total production of natural gas will have risen by another one-half compared to 2014.

This boom has effects on prices for consumers and profits for the industry. In recent years, electricity-generating companies in particular have led the "dash for gas" as their main fuel. During the recent **recession** of 2007–2008, natural gas use decreased, yet more natural gas was becoming available, so prices fell sharply. As the economy recovered, prices rose again, and some big users, even electricity generators, considered going back to coal. But over the long term, North America's natural gas industries look set to continue growing for at least another 40–50 years, with stores of this resource lasting for 250 years.

Hydraulic fracturing operation in North Dakota, in 2011.

TEXT-DEPENDENT QUESTIONS

1. Where was the first purpose-made natural gas well, and which gunsmith was involved?
2. How did the Bunsen burner affect uses of gas fuel?
3. Name three ways in which World War II helped to advance technology for making pipelines.

RESEARCH PROJECTS

1. Find out more about big industries setting up near natural gas and petroleum oil resources. Does this still continue today?
2. Gather more information about how the growing electricity network affected natural gas and petroleum oil. Did it affect the use of natural gas just for lighting, or for other uses, too?

Chapter Five

NATURAL GAS AND THE ENVIRONMENT

Burning fossil fuels—whether it's natural gas or any other type—releases huge amounts of carbon dioxide into the air. Carbon dioxide is regarded as a major so-called **greenhouse gas**. Rising levels of it help to trap and keep more heat from the Sun in Earth's atmosphere (the layer of air around the planet) and the oceans. This is known as *global warming*, and it is having enormous effects on the environment.

Words to Understand

emissions: substances given off by burning or similar chemical changes.

greenhouse gas: a gas that helps to trap and hold heat—much like the panes of glass in a greenhouse.

sustainable: able to carry on for a very long time, or at least for the foreseeable future.

Carbon dioxide levels in the atmosphere rose from about 320 parts per million in the Earth's atmosphere in 1960 to more than 400 parts per million in 2014. Nearly all scientists agree that this is the main cause of a rise in the average temperature of the atmosphere and sea surface. The average temperature has increased by about 1.5°F (0.9°C) in the past hundred years, and this trend is predicted to continue. Global warming is having massive effects on the Earth, including its long-term weather patterns, a process referred to as *climate change.*

Global warming and climate change have many far-reaching effects. Some kinds of natural habitats are shrinking, while others are spreading. The amount of carbon dioxide in the oceans is rising, making the water more acidic, which kills corals and other sea life. Glaciers and ice caps are melting, and the water they release adds to the increasing volume of the warming oceans to make sea levels rise—at present by about 1/8 inch (3 millimeters) per year. Over the next century, this could flood low-lying regions, where many of the world's people live, and where industry and farming occur. In many regions, weather is expected to be more extreme.

Good and Bad

Of the "Big Three" fossil fuels, natural gas burns "cleaner" than petroleum oil fuels or coal. That is, it makes less polluting substances. For the same electricity generated, natural gas releases, or emits, less than half as much carbon dioxide as coal. When burned in vehicles, it produces one-fifth less carbon dioxide **emissions** than does gasoline. Natural gas also produces less of other polluting substances, such as tiny particles and the sulfur- and nitrogen-containing gases that contribute to haze, smog, and stale air.

Natural gas has another role in global warming. It is composed mainly of methane, and methane itself is a very powerful greenhouse gas. In fact, for the same volume, it is 70 times more effective than carbon dioxide at causing the greenhouse effect. Methane does not last as long in the atmosphere, but over 100 years it is 25 times more powerful than carbon dioxide. So any release of methane makes a significant addition to global warming. From drilling for natural gas at the well, through processing, pipelines, LNG carriers and transport, to

LNG can be transported by pipeline or truck.

the end user, there are almost always some unavoidable leakages. These range from a claimed 1 percent in well-developed natural gas industries, such as North America's, to perhaps 10 percent in developing parts of the world. All of them affect global warming.

"Flare gas" is yet another problem. In the early years of petroleum oil drilling, natural gas was seen as a nuisance and simply set on fire, usually at the end of a stack or tower, called "flaring." This still occurs in North America at times—for example, as a safety measure when there is a sudden and unexpected rise in pressure from the

According to the World Bank, petroleum companies in the Niger Delta region of Africa flare off as much 17 billion cubic meters of natural gas—roughly equivalent to the annual consumption of Germany and France combined.

well. But in other parts of the world, natural gas is flared constantly because the well location is remote and there is no easy way to process it.

International laws are supposed to control flaring and force companies to gradually reduce the amount of gas that is leaked or flared. Even so, the amounts are still huge. This is not only a massive waste of energy, it's also another addition to global warming. One possible answer is to set up small GTL (gas–to-liquid) plants, as mentioned previously, at remote well sites. These would convert the natural gas to synthetic crude oil that could be sent along the existing oil pipeline or tanker vessel routes.

Natural Gas and Transport

Could natural gas become more important as a fuel for road vehicles and other transport? Scientific reports say that when all features are included—from drilling and extraction, to transport and liquefying, to building and maintaining engines—then, in terms of carbon dioxide emissions, there is not much difference between natural gas, gasoline, or diesel fuels. But what *would* cut carbon dioxide emissions by almost one-half would be to replace gasoline and diesel vehicles with electric ones that use power from a generator plant fuelled by natural gas.

Natural gas does not have the terrible and obvious environmental effects of, for example, a major oil spill. But there are still safety and environmental hazards associated with its production and use. Like oil wells, natural gas wells change the landscape. Fracking is a recent invention and no one knows the long-term effects after, say, one hundred years. But we do know that it uses huge amounts of water and chemicals, and produces plentiful waste fluids that need careful disposal at the surface.

The injected fluids and chemicals in fracking are usually thousands of feet below the surface. But, in theory and over time, they could seep and spread to affect the groundwater in rocks at shallower levels, and they could even affect wells and natural surface waters such as rivers and lakes. Also, changes in pressure and water content deep in the rocks could make them less stable and perhaps at risk of earth tremors or even earthquakes.

Safety and Disasters

North America has strict rules about transporting natural gas in pipelines, tankers, and pressure containers, and for storing it safely. Accidents still happen, however. Almost every year sees a significant natural gas leak, fire, or explosion. Leaks have many causes. These include problems at drill rigs and processing plants, old or rusty or cracked pipelines, faulty pumps and compressor stations, construction workers or even autos and aircraft hitting pipes, and also end-user boilers, furnaces, cookers, and similar equipment that are damaged or badly maintained.

Methane is heavier than air, so it tends to spread at ground level. Without its odorants, as mentioned earlier, it has no smell. Slow gas leaks can damage trees, birds, and other wildlife over a wide area. Sudden leaks have led to big fires and explosions, with great loss of life. In 1937, natural gas leaked and blew up a school in New London, Texas. Almost 300 students, teachers, and others died. This dreadful tragedy led to the rules on adding odorants to gas fuels. In 1944, on the East Side of Cleveland, Ohio, a liquefied natural gas storage tank sprang a leak, and the gas spread and seeped down into gutters, drains, and sewers. In the following series of explosions and fires, 130 people died and whole city blocks were demolished.

In Natchitoches, Louisiana in 1965, a pipeline explosion killed 17 people. A few years later, in 1968, a natural gas leak in Richmond, Indiana, set off fires and explosions in which 41 people died. These events led to new US rules about natural gas pipelines and equipment, known as the Natural Gas Pipeline Safety Act of 1968.

Recent Natural Gas Tragedies

- In 2011, a natural gas explosion and fire in Allentown, Pennsylvania, killed 5 people and destroyed several homes.
- In 2012, in Austin, Texas, 1 person died and another was injured in a house explosion due to a leaking natural gas main.
- In 2013, a pipeline natural gas compressor station in Tyler County, West Virginia, caught fire, and 2 workers died.
- In 2014, a natural gas leak was probably the cause of an explosion in apartment buildings in East Harlem, New York City, killing 8 people and injuring 70.

In 2004, the US government set up the Pipeline and Hazardous Materials Safety Administration (PHMSA) to ensure the natural gas network is as safe as possible, and that it affects the environment as little as possible.

In the 1970s, an oil and gas-drilling rig collapsed in Derweze, Turkmenistan. This resulted in a crater, nicknamed the Door to Hell, which has continued burning off natural gas for more than 40 years.

Methane Hydrates

Drilling in the deep sea means dealing with very low temperatures and extremely high pressures. These conditions favor the formation of methane hydrates, or fire ice, mentioned on page 15. This substance can clog machinery, and it can suddenly turn into methane gas and water inside the borehole, causing a sudden surge or even a blowout. Methane hydrate problems are well known at drill rigs, processing plants, pipelines, and other natural gas equipment.

The vast stores of natural methane hydrates in the deep seabed and under permafrost could be used as an energy source, as described earlier. Canada's methane hydrate reserves are estimated at between 5 and 20 times the amount of methane in the country's natural gas. Starting around 2000, Canadian and Japanese experts worked on safe ways of extracting the methane. However, in 2013, after spending $15 million, Canada decided to pull out, saying that shale natural gas was becoming more plentiful and less costly.

The United States, Japan, China, Norway, and other nations are exploring possible ways to extract methane from hydrates. The main method could be drilling, as in a regular natural gas well. But there are many big problems to overcome in technology and engineering. For example, the areas around the borehole may freeze, because as methane hydrate breaks up into water and methane, it draws heat from the surroundings. In addition, an underwater landslide triggered by a well could release

Natural Gas Timeline

The typical timeline for a new natural gas well is as follows:
- **Preparing to drill**. From 1 to 3 months are needed for tests, permits, legal matters, and to arrange for the drill equipment, crews, and supplies.
- **Drilling.** From 1 to 2 months are required for rig work, including setting up the drill rig, boring, steel casings, and cementing.
- **Fracking.** It takes 2 to 6 days to pump in the high-pressure fracking fluid, while also checking progress and flow rates.
- **Production.** In general, a well will produce gas for 25 to 40 years.

Most surface equipment is then taken away, apart from the wellhead valves, tubes, meters, and safety preventers, as well as pipes to the local gas lines.

Natural gas could be burned to power electric cars, like this one in Portland.

deep methane hydrates, which would allow vast quantities of methane to bubble up into the atmosphere.

A Bridge to the Future

Natural gas is often called a "bridge" fuel. That is, it could bridge the transition between fossil fuels, with their carbon dioxide emissions and many other problems, and a future of cleaner, **sustainable,** and renewable energy sources such as wind, solar, hydropower, and others.

Natural gas has several positive features. It burns less "dirty" than coal or petroleum oil fuels like gasoline. There is enough of it to last a long time, and its supplies are increasing, especially in North America. A future important role of natural gas in transport, for example, could be to burn it in generator plants that provide power for electric cars. Another role might be using methane to make the gas hydrogen to use as hydrogen fuel cells in future vehicles. This technology has a long way to go to be useful, however.

But, like other fossil fuels, natural gas has many negatives. Its reserves, even with advances like horizontal drilling and fracking, are limited. Burning it adds greatly to global warming, as do natural gas leaks—which also lead to danger, fires, and explosions. If natural gas (methane) leaks rise above about 3–5 percent, then, in terms of adding to global warming, this makes burning natural gas about the same as burning coal. No one knows the long-term effects of fracking, and many oppose this technology because of the possible risks from the chemicals used and the unknown effects on the rock formations under the ground. Extracting methane from deep-sea methane hydrates is an enormous challenge for technology and could trigger a global warming disaster.

However the natural gas industry develops, even as a "clean bridge to a renewable future," it will have major effects. This hugely important natural energy source affects the environment, climate change, land and water resources, wildlife, transport, power generation, public health and safety, and people's daily lives.

Natural gas can be obtained from deep-water drilling.

TEXT-DEPENDENT QUESTIONS

1. What is flare gas?
2. List five possible hazards of fracking.
3. Why is natural gas called a "bridge" fuel?

RESEARCH PROJECTS

1. Find out more about why natural gas is a "cleaner" fuel than coal or gasoline and diesel. Are the chemical reactions of combustion the same?
2. Look up information on the so-called hydrogen economy, including how natural gas and methane are involved.

"To waste, to destroy, our natural resources, to skin and exhaust the land instead of using it so as to increase its usefulness, will result in undermining in the days of our children the very prosperity which we ought by right to hand down to them amplified and developed."

—Theodore Roosevelt
President of the United States (1901 to 1909)
Seventh Annual Message
December 3, 1907

Further Reading

BOOKS

Doeden, Matt. *Finding Out about Coal, Oil, and Natural Gas.* Searchlight Books What Are Energy Sources? Minneapolis, MN: Lerner Publications, 2014.

Gogerly, Liz. *Fossil Fuels.* A World After. Chicago: Heinemann, 2014.

Hillstrom, Kevin. *Fracking.* Hot Topics. Detroit: Lucent Books, 2013.

Horn, Geoffrey M., and Debra Voege. *Coal, Oil, and Natural Gas.* Energy Today. New York: Chelsea House, 2010.

Marcovitz, Hal. *What Is the Future of Fossil Fuels? Future of Renewable Energy.* San Diego, CA: ReferencePoint Press, 2013.

Royston, Angela. *The Race to Survive Climate Change.* World in Crisis. New York: Rosen Classroom, 2014.

Zemlicka, Shannon. *From Oil to Gas.* Start to Finish, Second Series. Minneapolis, MN: Lerner Publications, 2013.

ONLINE

Energy Kids. "Natural Gas Basics." US Energy Information Administration. http://www.eia.gov/kids/energy.cfm?page=natural_gas_home-basics.

Hodgson, Susan F. "Oil & Gas in California." California Department of Conservation, Division of Oil, Gas, & Geothermal Resources. http://www.conservation.ca.gov/dog/kids_teachers/tr34/Pages/tr34pg1.aspx.

Oklahoma's Oil and Natural Gas. "Industry." http://www.oerb.com/?tabid=242.

Series Glossary

alloy: mixture of two or more metals.

alluvial: relating to soil that is deposited by running water.

aquicludes: layers of rocks through which groundwater cannot flow.

aquifer: an underground water source.

archeologists: scientists who study ancient cultures by examining their material remains, such as buildings, tools, and other artifacts.

biodegradable: the process by which bacteria and organisms naturally break down a substance.

biodiversity: the variety of life; all the living things in an area, or on Earth on the whole.

by-product: a substance or material that is not the main desired product of a process but happens to be made along the way.

carbon: a pure chemical substance or element, symbol C, found in great amounts in living and once-living things.

catalyst: a substance that speeds up a chemical change or reaction that would otherwise happen slowly, if at all.

commodity: an item that is bought and sold.

compound: two or more elements chemically bound together.

constituent: ingredient; one of the parts of a whole.

contaminated: polluted with harmful substances.

convection: circular motion of a liquid or gas resulting from temperature differences.

corrosion: the slow destruction of metal by various chemical processes.

dredge: a machine that can remove material from under water.

emissions: substances given off by burning or similar chemical changes.

excavator: a machine, usually with one or more toothed wheels or buckets that digs material out of the ground.

flue gases: gases produced by burning and other processes that come out of flues, stacks, chimneys, and similar outlets.

forges: makes or shapes metal by heating it in furnaces or beating or hammering it.

fossil fuels: sources of fuel, such as oil and coal, that contain carbon and come from the decomposed remains of prehistoric plants and animals.

fracking: shorthand for hydraulic fracturing, a method of extracting gas and oil from rocks.

fusion: energy generated by joining two or more atoms.

geologists: scientists who study Earth's structure or that of another planet.

greenhouse gas: a gas that helps to trap and hold heat—much like the panes of glass in a greenhouse.

hydrocarbon: a substance containing only the pure chemical substances, or elements, carbon and hydrogen.

hydrologic cycle: events in which water vapor condenses and falls to the surface as rain, snow, or sleet, and then evaporates and returns to the atmosphere.

indigenous: growing or living naturally in a particular region or environment.

inorganic: compound of minerals rather than living material.

kerogens: a variety of substances formed when once-living things decayed and broke down, on the way to becoming natural gas or oil.

leachate: liquid containing wastes.

mineralogists: scientists who study minerals and how to classify, locate, and distinguish them.

nonrenewable resources: natural resources that are not replenished over time; these exist in fixed, limited supplies.

ore: naturally occurring mineral from which metal can be extracted.

ozone: a form of oxygen containing three atoms of oxygen in a molecule.

porous: allowing a liquid to seep or soak through small holes and channels.

primordial: existing at the beginning of time.

producer gas: a gas created ("produced") by industrial rather than natural means.

reclamation: returning something to its former state.

reducing agent: a substance that decreases another substance in a chemical reaction.

refine: to make something purer, or separate it into its various parts.

remote sensing: detecting and gathering information from a distance, for example, when satellites in space measure air and ground temperature below.

renewable: a substance that can be made, or a process used, again and again.

reserves: amounts in store, which can be used in the future.

runoff: water not absorbed by the soil that flows into lakes, streams, rivers, and oceans.

seismology: the study of waves, as vibrations or "shaking," that pass through the Earth's rocks, soils, and other structures.

sequestration: storing or taking something to keep it for a time.

shaft: a vertical passage that gives miners access to mine.

sluice: artificial water channel that is controlled by a value or gate.

slurry: a mixture of water and a solid that can't be dissolved.

smelting: the act of separating metal from rock by melting it at high temperatures

subsidence: the sinking down of land resulting from natural shifts or human activities.

sustainable: able to carry on for a very long time, at least the foreseeable future.

synthesis: making or producing something by adding substances together.

tailing: the waste product left over after ore has been extracted from rock.

tectonic: relating to the structure and movement of the earth's crust.

watercourse: a channel along which water flows, such as a brook, creek, or river.

Index

(page numbers in *italics* refer to photographs and illustrations)

About the Author

Steve Parker is an author and editor of children's non-fiction books and websites, chiefly in the areas of nature and the biological sciences. He has written more than 100 titles about the natural world, animals and plants, ecology, conservation, rocks and fossils, mineral wealth, and Earth's varied and valuable resources—and how human activities are affecting them, both historically and into the future. Steve's recent works include the *Animal Diaries* series (QED, London) about how our exploitation of land, water, air and the general environment affects the daily lives of creatures as diverse as a garden spider, lion, penguin, golden eagle and shark.

Photo Credits

Cover
Clockwise from left: Dollar Photo Club/TTstudio; Dollar Photo Club/phant; Dollar Photo Club/Chepko Danil; Dollar Photo Club/nmann77; Dollar Photo Club/Jeff; Dollar Photo Club/Leonid Ikan; iStock.com/Stefan90.

Interior
Dollar Photo Club: 54 marcobir.
iStock.com: 12 CedarWings; 18 Dizzo; 23 photographer3431; 25 34 Westphalia; 29 Ron_Thomas; 30 tab1962; 33 sgoodwin4813; 35 AlbertPego; 39 IPGGutenbergUKLtd; 48 halbergman; 53 andipantz.
Library of Congress: 42.
NASA: 15.
US Navy: 26.
Wikimedia Commons: 10 Gordon T. Taylor Stony Brook University; 13 Daniel Foster; 14 Lvklock; 20 Erik Christensen; 22 Antandrus; 40 Tim Evanson; 43 Joshua Doubek; 47 Jukka Isokoski; 51 flydime.